I'm Your Huckleberry

poems

Erika Jo Brown

I'm Your Huckleberry

poems

Erika Jo Brown

Brooklyn Arts Press · New York

I'm Your Huckleberry
© 2014 Erika Jo Brown

ISBN-13: 978-1-936767-32-8

Cover design by Bethany Robertson. Interior by Joe Pan.

Published in The United States of America by:
Brooklyn Arts Press
154 N 9th St #1
Brooklyn, NY 11249
www.BrooklynArtsPress.com
info@BrooklynArtsPress.com

Distributed to the trade by Small Press Distribution / SPD
www.spdbooks.org

Library of Congress Cataloging-in-Publication Data

Brown, Erika Jo.
  [Poems. Selections]
I'm your huckleberry / by Erika Jo Brown. -- First edition.
    pages cm.
 Summary: "The debut collection of poetry from Erika Jo Brown" --
Provided by publisher.
  ISBN 978-1-936767-32-8 (pbk. : alk. paper)
  1. Poetry. I. Title.

PS3602.R6976A6 2014
811'.6--dc23
                          2014017861

First Edition, 2nd Printing

CONTENTS

IV.

V.

I'm Your Huckleberry

CAPTAIN SNUGZ RIDES AGAIN AGAIN

Break a brandy snifter. Break any
small thing. A nugget of bituminous
coal. Not a heart. Not a lot. Afterwards,
improve yourself. Refrain from hitting
snooze. Fix a small thing. A bug or
capillary. Eat a schnitzel with capers.
Stop taking orders. Adopt a schnauzer.
Adopt a funny German accent when
commanding it to stay. Captain Snugz,
how is your mouth always so hot?
I love you more every day, not less
and this concerns me. You mug. Plus,
we live on a floodplain. It may all seem
non-germaine but G-d, sometimes
it's cloudy, sometimes luminous.

DIRTY BIRDIES

For my rabbity heart, nervous in the
birches, I enrolled in a class for those
with pain or injury, but it wasn't
what I expected. A whiffle of light still
flickers by the wharf. Once, I was adopted
by a family of line dancers. When you fall
in love, then you are just down like debris,
a meteorite. Consider welding—to unite
by heat or compression, after softening.
Consider the silliness of yon weft
without a warp. What a weave we make.

Wether, you are a castrated ram. Whelp,
you are a young pup. Whether introduces
an alternative clause followed by another
alternative or not, or not. Cave paintings
existed during the first ice age. Your problems
are not new, although yes, it is cold in here.

Oh, counterfeit wampum! I saw the sign and it
said, VARICOSE VEINS DEMAND EXCELLENCE.
What are your demands? Consider how she
whimpers when you unpeel the sheet music.
Whoop, there it is. The foam-crusted waves
are also known as white horses. Don't mind
the noise, it's just birds loosing into the night.

SOMETIMES STARS SHOOT
FROM MY BREAST

I am a hen scattering feed
around my house for you
who's seen me aflutter
over rhubarbs, ridiculous cocks.
You're an alcoholic and
I'm a cockatiel, your lack plus
my surfeit makes an integer.
It's math, it's a small chicken.
Let us chuck this starling
darling, never be lonely.
I look towards the horizon
while you, too laden with grain
to pray, you must find another orison.
But rook, song-belcher, this season.

GNOMON

Sometime in the winter of our lives,
I was all about tillage. An operation,
a practice, an art of little trenches.
Tell me about it. The season provided
its best sledge. I had not one pretty
tile to tickle me, with the exception
of a Turkish repro, from Israel actually,
a gift from my absent auntie. These lacks
were tugging, as tilapia does a line alive.
My ticker was rendered pointless, more
or less. There was a sadness no leopard
could dispossess. But for the repetitive
ticks of a tractor I heard this summer.

This is my Monday sad day triage
poem. My sad cabbage in Monday
pottage poem. Sounds from an acreage,
like a made-up plot device. Like a
sparkly beverage. From a crow's eye,
there is no progress. Love's test
is actually a common everlasting native
to eastern North America. Things like
this. The spillage and the mileage. The
carriage through these blah blah blues.

ALONE IN THE SHOWER
I PRACTICE PEEING
LONG DISTANCES

A modicum of tenderness is necessary
but ill-appropriate here. Our origins
are errant. The same old ghost
stories do not repopulate the present.
Sand dulls everything.

I lack the leisure to be rude
when conditions are crude. I've rituals
too, that unravel if you learn them.

I've touched a million things.
Fingerpads are a site of memory,
of feathery jeopardy, of treachery.
People tell me about mine all the time
in succor. I know, I say, look, there's
a future and it's a vast expanse of desert
with lightning. And I can't always find
the oasis. And you can't always find the oasis.

Put up your fingerpad. Tell me which way
the wind is blowing. I'll start a repository
of touch memory, bound in clean paper.

I don't know why my body malfunctions
in comfort, but in the wilderness
I am a fucking ibex, sinewy and hard-
scrabbling, avoiding scorpions, trying
new roots. You can't choose delight, you
must walk outside and wait for it to find you.

FRENCH NEW WAVE CINEMA

Because I don't care for Godard,
I am the loneliest poet. Go,
dart, to the heart of my beloved.

Tell him: we mythologize each
other when we're apart. Tell
him: I'm a bit of a tweaker. No,

I don't actually *sleep* with
deers out here. Check yo
navigational chart. In fact,

a perfectly respectable club jam
came on the radio today. Tell him:
I'm sorry for accidentally kicking him

in the gonads. It's too bad, too,
I had imagined us on a gondola
in a scenic place funded carte blanche

with affection. Tell him: I don't do
goulash without meat. Tell him: of my love
for gorgonzola cheese: garbanzos.

Tell him: of my objectionable
tartness. Don't forget that part.
My goal is to go steady.

Although I'm rather cerebral,
I don't know shit about
beer. The avant-garde won't

protect me here. If I need you,
I know you'll be available to hold
my mitten on a starry evening. Oh,

tell my love nothing. I'll do it myself.

FAERIES

We have named the names but still
our capacity for desire and
sorrow is like a grand hotel.

This day was like cigarette ash
on the porch of a wild friend
whom in dreams you seize
and forcefeed sparkle cake.

On the porch also, faint memories
of undined wishes
like the flaccid nub of a party hat.

We see the good students
walking to the park in the sheer
cacophony of spring being nearly sprung.
Touch it.
The dancers wait for no thumb.

VIOLET IS A LADYPLANT WHOSE NEED FOR RAIN AND SUN REIGNS VIOLENTLY.

See, Violet, the ladyplant prefers
simplicity, the vinaigrette, the matching
of components indivisible and weak,
like starlings and sky, the villainous
sky towards which she reaches.
Vinyasana helps. She vibrates
when her little islet feels overly
pliant. She fancies herself a Vidalia
onion aguing a vindaloo stew or
a nice vichyssoise on her few
good days. Those inviolate
good days, when she doesn't feel
vicarious, an invalid, invalid,
a victim. When a mundane item,
a hydrant, for instance, resists
becoming something violent,
a trident with evil intent, for
instance. Mightn't she enjoy pollen
riven by the gem cutter above?
Things as themselves: angular,
faceted, sugar. Sweet Guadeloupe.
Vile vines creep 'round her planty mind.

PILOT PROTOCOL

In turbulence, there is no Kareem Abdul
Jabbar. Sometimes your eyes are glassy,
sometimes cloudy. When you see your
dead pet on the ped mall, you must act
similarly to when you've had a bad day
in the sky. Refrain from acid, though
the wondrous fountains of, I don't
know, chocolate, or better still, salty
caramel ice cream goo, might seem
ideal, they're apt to make you keel.
Trust me, I've been there. I've been
an ornament to success, despair, and
feathery ennui. Just keep the plane up.

HALF-NELSON

Somewhere, an actual balloon floats into the horizon
of a Midwestern town. I know that because I see it.
Everyone is sad. I know that because I talk to people.
Smart people are good at schematizing sorrow
in ravishing models. Somewhere, the whale-like
thrumming of French hip-hop thrums. Someone
has left a tissue in their pocket that sneezes
all over the new load of wash. General fruit
is not appealing, but three young apricots before
you, well. Please accept this half-ditty, half-prayer.
For once, it's not pity I'm after, just beauty.
There is no transaction like this. Forgive
my being forward at the end—rain hitting
a pane, canary-yellow, chai. Try it with me now.

II.

YOUR BODY, A-Z

A is for alfalfa Valhalla. B is for
banana bandana. C is for crème
cabanna. D is for you know what
D is for.

E is for tell me something I don't know,
you mathematical constant, you symbol.
Silent, you strengthen, you lead the eunoia.
Most common, your glyph was a little man
praying, amen.

F is for goodbye my fancy.
Fuck this apocalyptic diet.
In a figurative sense. And
for fancy dancing as catharsis.

G is for goodbye! wet winter socks.
An Artic fox among the flox, she titters,
a Nova Scotia splinter in midwinter.

H is for ham. My man is a ham
with cheese. We pretend kiss
in a dramatic style, then we
real kiss on real boardwalks.
G-d looked down and said,
give that girl a ham to make
a sandwich. And it was good.

I is for I don't get your poem.

J
K

L is for the way you look at me.
La la-la la-la la-la
la la.

M is for money. I don't have any.
$ is a symbol. Menus are
symbolic. I happen to like
exotic vegetables with farfalle.
Sue me for my nothings. My
kitchen is as fresh as a mature
daisy. My money troubles are
sharp like heartburn
in the throat. No.
My money troubles
result in heartburn in the
throat. Little evil mmmm.

N
O

P is for prosciutto.

P is for powerful jaws of powerful
dogs snapping on a rib-red Frisbee
as pollen parachutes to the ground
in a puff of fluff. Two Pinschers
in my purview, a doubled comfort
for a troubled mind. Were it smooth as this grass
with its snags of uneven pitches
and the whole people lying upon it.

Q is for qwying out loud
if qwerty is a wordy in *Words
With Friends*, then I'm the
queer queen of ice qweam.

R is for the ruffly apron I wear to wash
dishes. My man comes in with a briefcase
after a long night of teaching on video.
The kiss is perfunctory and I
listen to positivity tapes. So Plathy,
so laughy, as I riff off the rafters.

S is for let us now celebrate shorts.
Shucks. The shaggy sheik shrieked
for his shuttlecock as shrimp-eaters
shake with shame, slaked their claim
to clams. Calmly, a Shakespearean
actor, life a'shamble, shalommed
his reflection in the shaving mirror,
resolved to upgrade from shingled
shed to seaside shanty. A Shanghaied
shamus shimmied into a new sham,
between some new gams. Similarly,
a Shetland shepherdess prepped some
shimmery sherbet. All were relatively
little in stature. All came up with too
few stocks in hand. All preferred knee-
length trousers. A film about their lives
will be shewn at your local film festival,
where shortbread will be swerved,
as a shallot grows wildly by.

T is for thoughts are like invisible
farts and for times when Tourettic
rappers shout "squad!" which I
replace with "squab!" for my own
purposes. And P really is for prosciutto.

U is for um, uvula. La grand dame
louver, look, I'm so close to the edge,
I heart you, j'adore, my affection,
my affliction, even the letter is deviant,

starting all diagonal then staying all
diagonal, oh I shall not spell it out.
Cold acrosticker, I will meet you
halfway, love, no more.

V is for bring back uvula.
Vamoose, vile vices. Voila!

W is for I'm all-woman. I'm all
womb, man. I'm like, woo! Man!
I really am.

X is for excrement, duh. The Gambino
exit. Pooping is the necessary stepchild
of all bodily functions. It makes the gala,
spritzing sphincter sprinkles.

You are so bad. You ripple a nun's wimple,
you make eyes at almost whomever.

Zomegerd.

COOKING TO THE CAN-CAN

Contrary to popular belief, buckwheat
is not a wheat at all, but a member of
the rhubarb, rhubarb, peas and carrots
family. Contrary to popular belief, love
is not an emotion but a meaty agenda
with a dash of petite peppery treats.

Let him touch your pink peppercorn
and confuse your convection confection.
Folded, as blinis, feelings get complex
and squishy. Old wives say travel to
find the prized can of cannellinis.

Love can't be reduced like so many
consommés into a conceit. My love
is a quirky two-piece band from Nashville.
It will remind you of things that you like.

MAKING LIFE BETTER
AS WE LIVE IT

Say again that my eyes are
auriferous. Like hazel darts
of knowledge on this bitch.
In South Africa, a necklace
is a tire placed round the neck
and lit. A necklace is a chain
of events. An aubergine is an
eggplant in England but no
thing here. To auscultate is to
listen to internal organs. Your
belly is simply symphonic.
My neck is an orchard. What
was once a cupboard becomes
an aumbry in the right kind
of church. When you know
what you know what I'll
tell you I found in a book.
You need me. And I love you
too, nerd. Say again about
my nape, how it's your nectar.
Neutrinos have a specified spin,
but not much else. A lexical
negligee. That needle of desire
and daily chores and death.

LET'S ASSUME WE ARE EACH OTHER'S BEST BLUSHING BRIDES

My answers are lilies, puns, and yes
I say yes in many modulations, and
I'd like to try each one out
on you until your answer is
also yes, I would like you to drive
thousands of miles, shut off your
searchlights while I am sleeping
hot and in my yellow muumuu
and I will lift the covers to let you
in and I will promise not to open
my eyes and see the danger. As

a child, I learned that two
ex-wives are too too many
but like trigonometry I forgot
because facts have no practical
application in this life. I have trouble
sleeping well. As a skeptic
I don't go for the whole savior tip
but since there's you, there's a lot
I'm in distress about, such as this
giant ball of desire that sometimes
I dress up as stars to light your way

to me. If you drive thousands of
miles to hypothetically stand
next to me in the kitchen, then let's
have a dog, too. Yes, I've always been
fond of kousa dogwoods, please
let me know if there are any near
you, by bird or by hand.

WIND ADVISORY

Holy aioli, Aeolus is showing us
what's what. No one wins with
wind like this, except we can go
for breezy walks. On the highway
a sedan kisses a semi. Give us softer
wind, a zephyr from the west, fructifying
mangoes and whathaveyou. But our
lil' Greek god has thinned from his
strict diet of calamari and gin gimlets.

Thru the din, you know it's the boreas
boring thru the arras, the shaggy winter
wind. Be ruled. There are gusts and minor
chords, all of them shaking shit up. Be ruled.
As the song goes, a coltish tempest is gonna
come. You know this, like you know the invisible
conjoined twin on your frontal lobe, the one
who yells at your boyfriend when he brings
you flowers at the airport. The wunder-
kind glopping on the peanut butter.

The one who insists that catching 11:11
on a clock, digital or otherwise, indicates
the presence of angels encouraging you
to be more aware of patterns. Fine.
The chinook that shook the hinds of happiness,
&tc. And did you know that Zephyr
loved athletic Hyacinth so much he
killed him with a discus? These are
the winds that sank a bajillion ships.

SOME MEN KNOW ABOUT PATHOS

I can't blame you for fleeing a burning building,
you who smell like soap and milk and stability
and I know I shouldn't list in threes with

a rounding abstraction, but I've never been good
with words, such as when you told me
you were leaving me for Alice, the accountant,

and I lied that my ex was asking for me
back and you looked at me pitiably
as pitiable I was, in my pitiful white
tank top burnishing the autumn sunset.

I got on my bicycle. I bought organic dates.
I visited the autistic kid in my neighborhood
who stands in his front yard like an oracle,
whose mother regards me brusquely.

He told me about dogs: Great Danes (about
the size of him on all fours), Irish setters
(police dogs), and chihuahuas (friendly).

He never remembers me. If only we had just
information to go on! I know how to kick-
start a tractor, how to weld with a torch
and how to love some men.

SPACE

In ignorance, we find answers. In space, we find
frozen darkness, but also massive explosions
of mass slamming together. We don't know
what we find in space. Why I like to lie
so close to you. A base body pleasure,
a warmth we identify as our own. I know
nothing of constellations. Of freckled thighs.
We say give, as if it's a gift. Let us go
back to ringing descriptions of the unknowable.
You and space and you, as my need,
are replaceable, explosive, a moon tethered
to a fat planet. Venus has no moons. On Venus,
the sun rises in the west. If I say it, believe me.
Let us do a Lazarus, no. Resuscitations are only
miraculous when unaccountable. As you withdraw,
I find myself counting paces to your house.
It is a fortress of cheap plastic blinds, base.
How can a body orbit a home when the star
is absent? Dear me. The membranes
of my organs are dissolving, letting vital matter
bleed together. Tonight I prayed for rain
to withdraw into something larger.

ROBERT A. LEE
COMMUNITY CENTER

A bit of light glinted on the bottom
of the community pool. It said, think
of nothing. I said, what do you know
about Buddhist meditation and besides,
you can't even speak English. Now
you've dragged me into some pathetic
fallacy. It said, don't be a victim.
It oscillated like a heart monitor.
It made some new agey patterns
I forgot. I thought about cots on yachts.
Nothing. The light had moved
to higher ground on the lip. I felt lucky
to get a side lane. I complained that
I felt headachy. I said, I feel stick
pains. It didn't respond *si vous plait*.
It wasn't dead, but it was twilight.

CHICKABEE

When you're not here duct tape gets futzed
in my hair and by you, I mean everyone &
I am trying to block the artifacts & bland-
ishments of loss & love & remember
as a kid, *all things bright & beautiful*
appeared on my nightstand & I believed
in magic, not these tit-for-tat gestures
but some people are burning. Some people
are all aflame.

III.

DEAR ONE

I would like to express my affection for you
by talking about myself. This is already underway
and feels wrong. Mister frog eyes and your croaking.
People are giggling about your proclamations
again. When I traced the map of Africa I wanted
to learn about boundaries and win at Jeopardy.
I've always gotten off with bad behaviors. The
first thing I think about in the morning is a sort
of despair that tracks thru my day like a search
dog with muddy paws. Pause to take in spiders.
Be at heart, dear arachnids. Metafwog is here.

CRUSOE IN LOVE

(AFTER BISHOP)

It happens like this. Maybe I've drifted
on driftwood or batted about several islands
where poisonous blossoms bloom
seductively for a bosun ill-equipt, if not
downright toxic then lacking garlicky
nourishment, so I moved on, zagging
perilous seas until I landed here.

Or, I imagine us together on an island
with goats & berries & scrappy vinelands
based on some time stuck together in
traffic. Well, that's what imagination is
for and we'll need it on our island.
We'll need survival skills, but also to face
facts. How would we look marooned?
I feel you'd face my hair, the sea
with utmost bravery. Say *we'll need.*

There are other niggling questions. Where
could we find such an island? This universe is
made of bright cities, pocket shops, seasoned
crops, glottal stops and we can't hide from our
creators' eyes, no matter who is playing Crusoe.

But I've no use for lack of will & I suspect you
don't either. It's up to us to survive
in muddy blinks, dying our wildstock
pink, sliding down basalt volcanoes on salty
arrears, falling in love with, really falling
in love with weekdays. Instead of recycled
love, we'd say *frogs and logs and polliwogs*
because they'd be all around us and little else.

We'd register flora & fauna, some sparse
hairs, the curvature of woman as traced by
smooth, flat fingers, the necessary branches
needed to start a fire for simple supper
of meat, roots, & succulents.

Which is a way of saying *come here*. I love
this island that we make.

GARDEN OF CAMAS

1.

The garden, my neighbor
tells me, is conceptually
real. It's a piece of dirt
in the ground. There
were instructions and
flirtations, and really
what is the difference?

My old man love, the
one with the vasectomy,
planted me a garden. I
fled to the mountains,
left him in the prairie
in early spring. The fields
were just about to birth
bread. I know nothing
about midwivery, but feel
pregnant all of the time.

2.

Actually, I know about standing
and I know about water. Saying
I hope you breed is diff'rent
from noting twin-bearing
hips, but we're still talking.

My sentiment grows havisham.
It is set in its ways and creepy.

It is cause for célèbre and occasionally
requires literary references.

There is no generating principle, is
there? How I wish for order
that is cyclical, but lately I find
myself turning more and more to you.

3.

A friend advises, don't put
out 'til the butterleaf sprouts
and my favorite neon sigh
he says, is the urban equivalent
of a hawk circling

                                      bodies in water.
When I was younger, me and
a couple of lesbians toplessly
ploughed a small acreage,
divided distinct plots, tilled
alternatively. Gave it some time.

4.

My friends here in this temporary
home, we have grown like tendrils,
vegetal with ampersands and
overgrown affinities. We rub
against each other like
cilantro and marigolds.

Rolling in the alfalfa
never happened. All the same
nostalgia grows like a path
cut through clod and marl.

SPUR THE THRESHOLD

The machine has some of function,
we don't know. It's easy, simple really,
to get caught up in lattice and gingerbread,
missing Gesamtkunstwerk for the fretwork.
This is not a place for grand revelations,
insulated as it is. There is a house,
then a block, then a city, and G-d,
one could get distracted. There is
an architect I know who prefers
to see structures at work: cogs,
pistons, pulleys, steam, the works.
The work is savoring the grain, not
minding the burls. People lose fingers
on lathes but go back to the wood.

SPIDEY, MAN

I cannot wait to see you again
and forthwith to kiss you again

and again. Generic prairie buds
are practically exploding in anticipation.

A fucking headache, if I'm honest.
Oh pheasant, I'm thinking about

conservation and hunting and
our little house in the suburbs

sagely colored, covered with sage
where we use each other like gasoline.

I don't burn for you as much as
I saw a dead and dried spider in

a borrowed cereal bowl. I blew it
out of the door. It strove straight

up. I wished you were here in
the ensuing silence, the stupefaction.

IV.

BETWEEN THE STATES

Summers in the south resolve to a dewy decimal
of garlands festooning historic ironwork
is what I might say if born on a monied Monday.
After a flurry of hurricanes my doggie does
cartwheels on pine needles is what I might say if
I'm being honest. Southerners are a droplet of due
on chinoiserie, cracking elaborate pasts on steel cut glass.
A cool pumpkin on plump skin, my canine and I
prefer fresh cut grass to drag our rumpus around,
to run from dark imaginings. This is not an indictment
of my dog or myself or anything the eye can peel.
Weddings in public squares are circular. A bride
walked down the processional to Al Green and
I kept walking renewed, you know.

BERNADETTE

Bernadette lights a cigarette,
sighing with regret how love
is like an egret, pecking each
step, a domestic pup zoned
in a zoo one mustn't repet.
She owed a debt to no one,
been ensnared in said
net, according to most inter-
pretations, though the threat
now was low, like a heat.

She felt cagey. She ranged,
fretting, this silly brunette.
She considered the chess set
next to the splashy gazette
complacent, a preset duet,
clinical, as if placed by pipette.
Bernadette sipped some anisette.
From her kitchenette, she thought
she heard midwestern minarets.

Forget this, thought Claudette,
observing our mousy Bernadette
futzing with tiny pink barrettes.
On the whole, she was elegant,
parried without becoming upset
but for pacing and some in-
sipid squats. She shifted,
sifting thru more sober
sobriquets. Restless, she set
out across Lafayette, pursuing
the echo-echo of yon silhouette.

LOVE IS THE PITS

Why start at the beginning of the day
or otherwise when I'd like to construct
the present as a present for you?
The chicken in my tupperware is sexier
for being the chicken in the tupperware
of the girl you are thinking of somewhere
squished between your hundreds of
meaningful correspondences. I'm sure
the courtship with your wife involved
cherry blossoms, but here we are separately
admiring regional flowers and we're
creating a cloud over the Midwest,

over tri-state areas. Others can't see
or I haven't checked but weather
is measurable like language and if I can
just keep tapering these words out
to reach you, you may feel a tingling
pinprick. And we're both engaged privately
but I slept with this image last night
of unwashed grapes, of the film, of
rinsing off detritus to reveal red
ripe globes, ready and touching.

THE PRESIDENT

The President demands all your golden
paperclips. The President demands your
nights, which is fine, because she's the
President. The President already has
your hay-sown days. You give the Pres-
ident your children, one after another.
The President has established connection
with your umbilical cord, which she
tugs at random, sending you careening
back to the President. You have come
all this way for the President. The
President is a lady of many stipulations.
You steal a few quiet moments with
her creamy cardstock. You know
that in the basement your hay fever
has much abated. Thanks to you, the
President, the chiggers and the sandfleas
are hardly a problem. The President
builds monuments to her nuclear
family and you write the memorandums.
Morals, don't come in to this, your
mouth stuffed with morels. The President
is a busy woman. You realize you are
being watched. You are being watched.

WE ALL CHOOSE
OUR ORGANIZATION

It's been an unusual October. Dumb deer
and their jumping louse agree. I found a dead
mouse in my bedroom, this mourning by
some silken blouses. The temperature spiked.
I grabbed some grapes and hiked beachward,
where I stripped to my underwear and under-
shirt. The mouse was being ferried to the under-
world. I felt an ant in my underpants. A man
appeared in a black turtleneck, black slacks,
silver hair. I flicked my eyes away. He went
straight into the water and I wondered if he
was Baptist or crazy or what. Wetland under-
brush can contain all kinds of surprises. So too
can houses. An innocent room wherein all manners
of drama are played out. An innocent head
palmed in the hands of a spouse. I lost the man
but heard his lapping flaps. Pity the mouse.
My slippered steps like thunder, my boxed
cereal like plunder. Each thing a wonder.

LIGHT VERSE DEMANDS
RADIANT TURNS

For instance, there's a difference between a shadowy
geranium and one in full exposure, but what
does the speaker know about the sun or the function
of puns?
                    She is just trying to tell you about the loss
of leaves from her Japanese maple, turning seasons
for unobvious reasons. We've strayed again.

                                Lightness may contain
clandestine expressions, melancholic obsessions
trilling within us the saccharine squeamishness
of accepting butterscotch from old people.

Anecdotal digressions, images of nature, are all
just hands reaching out to build your worthpile
(breaching a particular solitude for the bookish
who can't stop looking at scorpion-shaped light).

ADUMBRATION
VIBRATION STATION

My shadow is a wimpy Zulu, a wholesome
Hebrew who recognizes owls by the sound
of their breaths. My shadow never ties its hair up,
it lets its hair down, it is made of bobbypins.

My shadow puts lists in its ears that
emit from its pits as only good
architecture can. It smells like ridiculous
mango, eats mothballs, ritualistically rhymes
bustle with muscle.

My shadow believes in the fingerpad,
has sensitive olfactory endings, explodes
with love. My shadow watches its shadow get
lost at night, lets its mouth pucker sour on the
hour after hour, then showers. OK.

My shadow is an astronaut, a porch sweeper,
it does not give a fuck about you, it suckles
the world. My shadow does not
titter over groin vaults, keeps meticulous cuticles.

This is not a safe place for us. There are
wolves on the corner. Wolves who don't know
where they are, who switch willy-nilly between showtunes
and power ballads. OK. We are shifting.
Something delicious and really tiny is going to happen.

My shadow has been locked for hours in a
furnitureless room, a funless zoom.
Kerbloom. It may've sounded more
caustic than I meant it, come back and
kiss me.

ABATTOIR

Being made tender like torture
or rather, little chordata, trace
the line of production, leading
where? Sniff the air, it smells
like fear. But you've seen the
workings of the mallets of the
French chefs a thousand times,
you ordered this dish.

DENTAPHRASE

Singing swing low, sweet chariot
coming for to carry me home,
I heard a distinct hiss
in the woods—this is not where
I tell you I saw a snake and
it was Satan or a mean child
hiding with a mean secret
to disrupt my singing—and I
sat on a soft termighty log
and let the dog drink straight
from my bottle, just as straight
from the bottle as I drink
the cheapest red wine when
I am playing a true fantasy
of my worst self, like the self
singing on a marshland path alone,
hearing but unable to interpret
the sounds, sibilant or toothsome.

V.

FIELD GUIDE TO TAILGRASS
PRAIRIE WILDFLOWERS

I'm sorry for using you, whorled
milkweed, large yellow lady's
slipper, field milkwort, obedient
plant, wild four o'clock, larkspur,
false pennyroyal, scurfy pea.

I read an aphorism or pop
song or military recruitment tract
that said our names are our
value. My boyfriend is called
BJ. Our imaginary dog is Señor
Huevos Brown-Love. I am
a small German flower. I too

think it's a shame we think
in language inherited or passed
along like cold sores or cold
sores blistering in the summer.
Really any other way to talk

about myself feels foolish
or fascistic. I have a great ass
if you like fat asses. Bees they
claim have no language but
who doesn't believe in the power
of drones over villages
at night? Something I believed

to be a cricket turned out to be
a burly twig. Chores is a word
we do at home and chillaxing
is what we do on vacation
once we get there which requires
infinitesimal exchanges. Did you

feed the fish? Did you leave
the paisley curtains askance so
robbers will not heist our house
so the idea let's burgle

that house because they are
away does not transpire? Because
we are not away. We are presently

present. Even if it appears
in our thinking as —haha the
dusting is manageable. Water
here tastes like shit but it's free.
So here's something beautiful

and real: I give you a regal eagle,
a sweaty chunk of cheddar
cheese. I do my best work as
a human on a bicycle. Just think
how I've used the names of flowers.

I've borrowed the thought of humans
late night as protection against
the beasties who materialize as names
with ghostie consonants. Just kidding,

you are my buddy. Unless, gentle peat
moss, you mean to suggest this
whole time I've been talking to myself.

DECIDEDLY LYRICAL

Her sleeves slapped in the breeze.
Little wheezes. Her sleeves slapped
like sails. Summer returned. She
sloped down a hill on her bicycle.
Her hair smellt of fire. Her hair
silty sweet. The fire smellt of
umami. Winter sledge begone.
In lack of slush she slaked her need
for ashen breath. For sherbet.
The night was warm. She heard
the sand of flapping slaughter
baddies of winter. In simpering
winds. No sleet but her hair
honeyed and bushy. The sound
of her sleeve slipping through
a path in space. In movement
a sliver. A sluice of a woman
audible, alone in the night.

LET'S DANCE

Like a Saladin salad, memory is built
on the unwashed bones of unbelievers.
All this worrying about the past is just
worrying about the future. Ain't that right,
panther? Isn't this the right place? It takes
a self-important person to salsa and tussle,
no, to make a grandiose statement, grand
as the piano I never learned to play, grand
as the Greek terrace on which I wept
over a lover. It takes any person
to make a statement, untarnished
and true. The stars are winking tonight.
Clouds have sidestepped this evening
to allow us swifter navigation. In truth, heather
will grow and weather is always, whether
we, small me, remembers to love it or not.

HAIL, NO

Tonight I peed in the church
for the first time. If you pee
in a church and no one's there,
do you still need to squat? Yes.

I took a cookie, overly spiced
midwesternly, what is this, ginger?
Nutmeg? At least I have a life
in which something to do with gratitude.

White robes are lined up in the hall
looking like angels. I am wearing
a baggy men's jacket. Jesus Christ,
how the sycamores shudder.

And how I am thirsty. The night
is laden with sycamores, lined up like
angels. Thirsty sycamores.

DEPRESSIVE NARCISSISM, OR THE CASE OF THE LYRICAL I, OR CAPERS ARE FOR BAGELS, OR WITNESS

Some mornings I'd like to get a witness, not because I think I'm deserving of some type of eternal reward, but rather because I'm like, damn, these bananas, look how yellow, what are we supposed to do, and why could I open the curtains yesterday but today it's different? And I'd like to think it's a function of loneliness, or nonsense, or narcissism masked as lonely nonsense, but it's the circuiting that's got me concerned. Just a person to watch me squeeze teabags, to watch me defrock, whom I can chide, and I used to think they were all love poems, because of their domestic qualities, but now I'm thinking that love poems are something else altogether. Watch me think.

SKINS

Language is skin we exchange sonically.
Hives develop with a warmth around the nape.

Ladybugs land on our chest and expire.
So let's lay supine, sausage-like, reading

separately how language is like skin.
Pruritus, the itching sensation broadly

splotches shins, fills a face with red wine.
Hives creep around ankles and hairlines.

Spider bites, bee stung lips, sunburn, rosacea,
scarlet fever, buboes, thin membranous organs.

Hives splay across thighs like a meteor shower;
language is a glittering assault, destroying its own evidence.

SHELLFISH

I like my history movies with reenactments and my science with CGI because I want it that way. Tell me why, m-m-mollusk must you lean and loaf, observing a blade of summer seaweed when there are rock lobsters endangered in coastal waterways. Don't be so shellfish. I wear my heart on the sleeve of my exoskeleton. I'm all inside out about it. I'm not one to make macro-critiques, but when you post upworthy videos without revealing the punchline, you are contributing to the click-bait problem. Aquaculture is the wave of the future. Over 40% of humans rely on the sea as their main source of protein. I'm allergic to self-pity, but I eat it all the time. You are so fresh, so protean, you salty bivalve. Urchin of the sea, but a freak in the sheets. Due to stylish consumption of oysters and other factors, more and more people are moving seaward. Soon, only Iowa will be left. Mussels with heavy metal content, prawns of arsenic, embrace me with your thousand claws. Tell me I'll never be lonely again.

EWED BETTER

Come smoke my superb sheepherb. But what
about your husbandry? And why were wizened
white men so fetishistic about shepherds anyway,
with their calendars and verdures and nymphs. And
have you herd bird is a word, among the glebes
and leas – feathered, winged, and bipedal – I mean,
waterfowl, plover, and petrels. In taxonomic language,
nightjars are rendered caprimulgiformes, rendered
with butter in Franciose's creole chicken kitchen.
Folkloric nightjars are crepuscular goatsuckers,
chloroforming Billy Capra, doing their untoward
dances undeterred. Goats browse, while sheep
prefer clover. Sheeps keep a stiff upper lip, split
by a groove – groove is in the heart, undergirded
by tobacci. What the flock has happened to this
fursome cur? Do you smell the distinctly nutty rutting
odors? And how many sheps have we heard?

SOY SOLUTIONS

So! This is where you've been hiding.
My beloved, a rob roy swigging mama's
boy, like a Helen of Troy, cloying, deploying
fancy dancing. Singing nightshade, night
shade and potatoes, eggplants and tobacco
all belong to each other in the solanum
genus. You know how sullen, just how
suddenly sodden things can get around
here, dummy. To say nothing of sorrow.
A soupçon of poutine is what you need
on a day like yesterday, I understand. I
on the other hand, feel my tingling tibias,
can hear sweet swampy sparrows like
sotto voce bossa nova. Oy vey. Le sigh.
Sorry I yelled when you just wanted to
poop bok choi. All in favor of charging
forth. Selves, raise your hands, say yes.

ACKNOWLEDGEMENTS

Thank you to my teachers: Jim Galvin, Patricia Spears Jones, Jonathan Monroe, Geoffrey Nutter, and Lyrae Van Clief-Stefanon.

Thank you to my homeslices: Hannah Arem, Micah Bateman, Aaron Belz, Becky Boyle, Thea Brown, Derek Gromadzki, A.C. Hawley, Hugh Hayden, Michele Hirsch, Matthew Klane, Benno Kling, Tina LaPerle, Tricia Lockwood, Sheila Maldonado, Tony Marra, Joe Pan, Jon Papas, Zach Powers, Isabelle Rostain, Bridget Sweeney, and Gale Marie Thompson.

Special thanks to my cuz, Jake Levine.

Thank you, family. This expresses but a modicum of my gratitude.

This book is for Love.

The author gratefully acknowledges the editors of the following publications where these poems first appeared, sometimes in different forms:

Anomalous Press
> Captain Snugz Rides Again Again
> Dirty Birdies
> The President

Back Room Live
> Faeries

cant
> Alone in the Shower I Practice Peeing Long Distances
> Spur the Threshold

Forklift, Ohio
> Let Us Assume We Are Each Other's Best Blushing Brides
> Sometimes Stars Shoot from My Breast
> Light Verse Demands Radiant Turns

H_NGM_N
> Depressive Narcissism, or The Case of the Lyrical I,
>   or Capers Are for Bagels, or Witness

Humble Humdrum Cotton Frock
> Decidedly Lyrical

ILK
> Making Life Better As We Live It

Jellyfish
> Between the States
> French New Wave Cinema

Petri Press
> Bernadette
> Violet is a ladyplant whose need for rain and sun
>   reigns violently.

Spork
> Hail, No
> Love is the Pits

Strange Cage
> Field Guide to Tallgrass Prairie Wildflowers

Transom
> French New Wave Cinema

Wave Press tumblr
> Wind Advisory

A limited edition broadside of "French New Wave Cinema" was printed by the University of Iowa Center for the Book in celebration of the 2012 Mission Creek Festival.

ABOUT THE POET

ERIKA JO BROWN is from New York. Her chapbook, *What a Lark!*, was published by Further Adventures Press in 2011. She was educated at Cornell University and the University of Iowa Writers' Workshop, where she was a Capote Fellow in Poetry. Most recently, Brown taught at Savannah State University and co-curated the Seersucker Shots reading series. Brown is currently a PhD candidate in Literature and Creative Writing at the University of Houston.

BAP

Brooklyn Arts Press

Brooklyn Arts Press (BAP) is an independent house devoted to publishing poetry books, lyrical fiction, short fiction, novels, art monographs, chapbooks, translations, & nonfiction by emerging artists. We believe we serve our community best by publishing great works of varying aesthetics side by side, subverting the notion that writers & artists exist in vacuums, apart from the culture in which they reside and outside the realm & understanding of other camps & aesthetics. We believe experimentation & innovation, arriving by way of given forms or new ones, make our culture greater through diversity of perspective, opinion, expression, & spirit.

Our staff is comprised of literary loyalists whose editorial resolve, time, effort, & expertise allows us to publish the best of the manuscripts we receive.

Visit us at BrooklynArtsPress.com

00063

Made in the USA
Charleston, SC
29 July 2015

44622324R